Bird Beaks

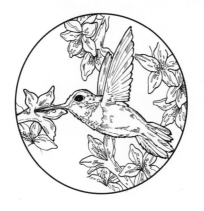

HOUGHTON MIFFLIN   BOSTON

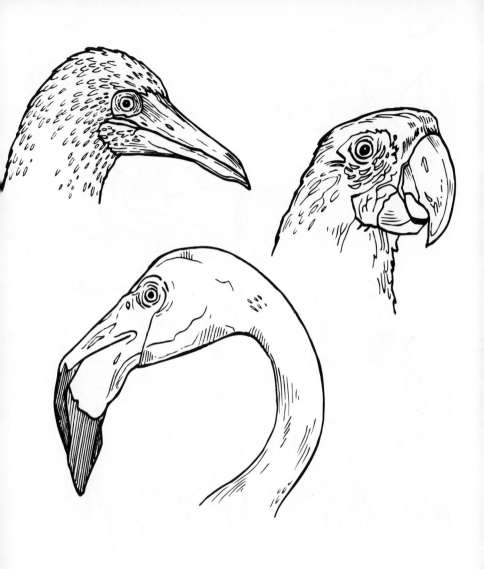

All birds have beaks.
Not all beaks are the same.

1

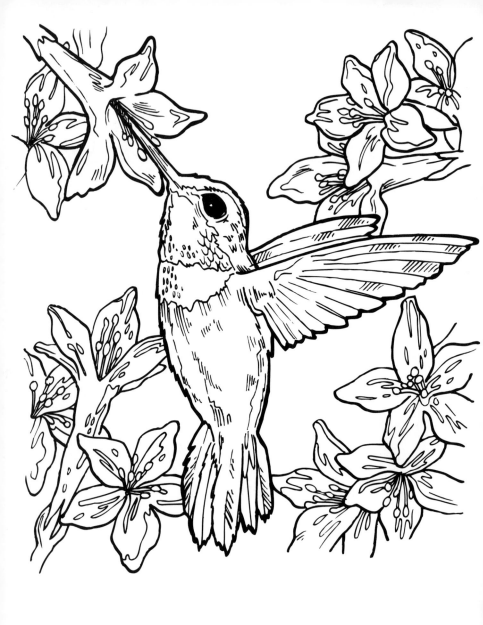

This bird has a thin beak.
It can suck food from flowers.

2

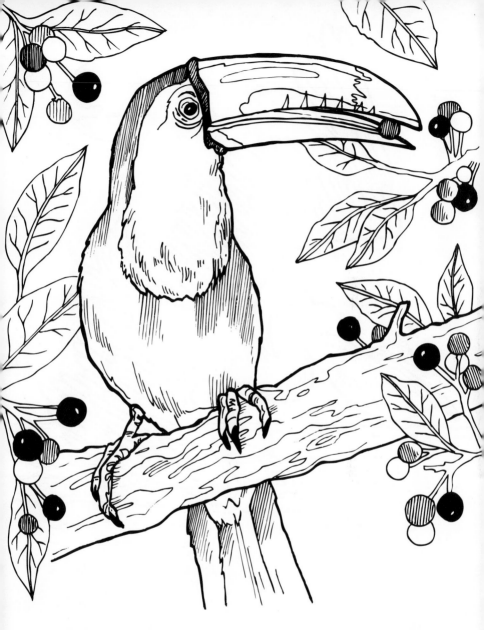

A beak like this can pick fruit.

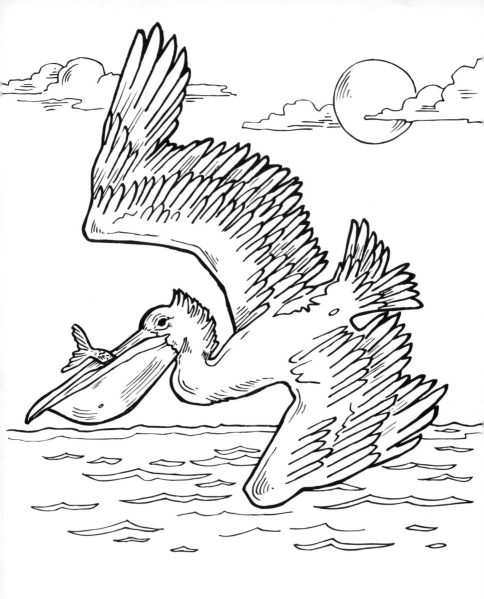

A beak can be like a fish net.
This bird will eat a lot of fish!

4